The Last Lie

Also by Tony Gloeggler

ONE ON ONE (Pearl Editions, 1999)

ONE WISH LEFT (Pavement Saw Press 2002, Second Edition, 2007)

MY OTHER LIFE (Jane Street Press, 2004)

GREATEST HITS (Pudding House Publications, 2009)

The Last Lie

Tony Gloeggler

The New York Quarterly Foundation, Inc.
New York, New York

NYQ Books™ is an imprint of The New York Quarterly Foundation, Inc.

The New York Quarterly Foundation, Inc.
P. O. Box 2015
Old Chelsea Station
New York, NY 10113

www.nyqbooks.org

First Edition

Set in New Baskerville

Layout and Design by Raymond P. Hammond
Cover photos by Tom Guiltinan

Library of Congress Control Number: 2009940956

ISBN: 978-1-935520-15-3

The Last Lie

Acknowledgments

Some of the poems in this collection appeared in the following journals: *Amicus, The Bridge, Graffiti Rag, The Ledge, Long Shot, The Massachusetts Review, The New York Quarterly, One Trick Pony, The Paterson Literary Review, Pearl, Poet Lore, Quercus, Rattle, Rhino, Skidrow Penthouse, Slipstream, Turnstile, Washington Square,* and the weekly newspaper feed *American Life in Poetry.*

A few of these poems also appeared online at poetz.com. "Crossing" was included in the chapbook *ONE ON ONE* (Pearl Editions, 1999) and a number of these poems were included in the chapbook *MY OTHER LIFE* (Jane Street Press, 2004).

I would especially like to thank William Packard of *The New York Quarterly* & Tim Monaghan of *The Ledge* who consistently supported my work when I first started sending out my poems.

Thanks to Raymond Hammond for doing all the work in putting this book together. Thanks to Michael Flanagan, Doug Collura and Ted Jonathan for reading these poems and telling me what they thought and felt. Thanks to Tom Guiltinan for taking the photos, Sophia LaTouche for riding the F train back and forth and being such a low maintenance model and her mom Elinor for letting her pose while hoping that her daughter will never read any of the poems.

This one's for Erica & Hilary & Suzanne.
For Joshua too.

Contents

The Last Lie

LITERATURE

Anytime anyone anywhere
mentions great literature
I think about my Uncle Dom,
his crutches and braces,
his throne-like chair padded
with lumps and strips of Styrofoam
molded around his polio, humped
like-a-boulder back and the wall
to wall bookcase that towered
behind it. With the top shelves
lined with hard-spined volumes
of Hemingway and Steinbeck,
he'd grab his nearest crutch,
maneuver it like a deli clerk
and pry, slide one book from
its slot, drop it into my arms
to read by next weekend.

Mostly I remember the paperbacks,
thirty-five cents each and tucked
in the bottom left hand corner
with big breasted women spread
across the covers and the first time
I jerked off. I was eleven and a half
and "Lust League" was my favorite.
Hank Crimson played center field,
hit clean up for the Mississippi Hens
while I leaned against the couch
with my legs stretched across
the carpet and my dungarees
unbuttoned. In odd chapters, Hank
pounded game winning doubles

into the gap or made perfect pegs
to nail sliding runners at the plate.
In the even ones, road trips ended
with Hank and the star attraction
of some strip club humping loudly
in a bathroom stall or Hank opening
his motel room door to find
the team owner's wife and virgin
daughter lying in his bed naked.

It wasn't too long before I walked
down stairs to the dimly lit basement
of my first girl-boy party, stood
in a circle watching a bottle spin
and took my first steps to maybe
someday getting laid and met
Regina Rowland in the middle.
I never thought about my uncle
sitting in his chair and reading,
watching all the girls walk beneath
his window in thin summer skirts
and tube tops. I never wondered
if he ever kissed a girl, felt her
mouth all over his tensed body,
sat back as she mounted him,
slid up and down until he closed
his eyes tight, made some kind
of wounded animal sound and came.

Me and my uncle never talked
about things like that. He died
before I ever wrote anything
I wasn't afraid to show people

and he never knew that I wanted
to write words that move people
like The Grapes Of Wrath and Lust
League, words that would open
your eyes wide, make you want
to go out and change the world,
make a quiet man take his hand,
his limp fingers and open his pants,
touch himself until he feels
like he was making love to,
fucking the trashiest, most
beautiful girl in the world.

NOT ME

If I was Billy Collins
I would sit and try
to write a poem
nearly every day.
The opening lines
might sound like
neighbors meeting
on a street corner,
neighbors who may
or may not know
each other by name.
They'd nod, talk
traffic, snow, heat,
baseball, maybe stop
walking, try to say
something clever,
tongue in cheek funny
with an easy rhythm
and subtle rhymes
riding down a summer slide
splashing in a pool
on the hottest day
of the year and maybe
right before walking
away, one would lean
in, mention a dead
Greek poet or the twin
towers in a voice
just above a whisper
and your eyes may mist
for half an instant.
But today, a woman

I've worked alongside
for fifteen years is lying
in a bed with liquid
in her lungs and cancer
in the liquid, a woman
nicer and kinder
than I could ever be
is lying down scared
and I'm not.

UNDERCOVER

Italian ladies draped in lace
placed coins in collection plates,
lit green novena candles.
German Shepherds sniffed
the wooden crutches, nuzzled
against my leg braces. Mothers
grabbed their children's hands,
whispered, "Don't stare."

When they walked away,
I flipped them the finger,
shut my eyes and turned
my braces into airplane wings,
my crutches into machine guns.
I swooped down, fired
round after round and flew
home with my thumbs raised.

I sat on our fire escape
making no sounds and trying
to blend into the background
like a spy. I imagined it was me
picking teams for stickball,
hitting Spaldeens two sewers long
and racing around the bases
like a skinny black kid.

Nighttime, I slipped under
the covers with a flashlight,
wrote in tiny notebooks. Careful
not to let my pencil scratch

against the paper. Afraid
someone could see that spec
of light, read my words. Afraid
they had ways to make me talk.

READING AND WRITING

A woman who may
or may not be dying
of cancer is reading
out loud from her novel
in progress to a small group
of friends and acquaintances
at a West Village coffee shop.
Later, you overhear different
people say she looks good,
wonder if she's wearing a wig,
maybe too much make-up.
The last time you talked,
she said she saw everything
different now, figured
out what was important:
herself, family, friends, herself
in an occasionally shifting
order, and writing,
writing every day.

You went home early,
disappointed, sad. Nothing
she read stepped on
the subway with you,
leaned over, whispered
into your ear anything
that made a difference.
You were still alone, a bit
cold, still feeling sorry
for yourself and acting
like you were lost. After
you tossed your jacket

on the couch, boiled water
for tea, you sat down, picked
up a pen and wrote this,
then read it twice and knew
it couldn't help anyone either,
and everyone, especially you,
is dying every day anyway.

CATHOLIC SCHOOL

I look her over
through the peephole:
Navy blue blazer, gold
crucifix, plaid skirt,
white knee socks.
Safe. I crack open
the door. She steps back
the way Claire Kerchoff first did
when it was her turn to spin
the bottle and it stopped,
pointed to me. Everyone
made sloppy sucking sounds
as we met in the middle
of the circle to kiss.

This one is selling candy.
A dollar a bar. I smile,
flash my sweet tooth, open
the door wider, invite her in.
I'll take two with almonds,
two pure chocolate, two
peanut crunches, two
with cashews and raisins.
Wait here. I get my wallet
from the bedroom, count
out the bills into her open
hand. One. Two. Three. Four.

I want to ask her
if the little boys and girls
still sit in alternate rows.
Do the dumb ones

still sit in the back
near the coat closets?
Does Sister Christine still
strut up and down the aisles?
Will she smack the back
of my head every time
she catches my hand
in my pants pocket?
Will she march me
to the front of the room,
make me place both hands
on the top of her desk
—"I said flat, Mister"—
swing her arm back
and whack my hands
with a thick gold ruler
until my fingers ring
like an air raid drill?

Five. Six. Seven. Eight.
She smiles and thanks me,
wishes me a nice day.
I lock the door, lie down
and think about her blonde
bangs, button nose, pink
tongue, her wet lips
while I eat my chocolate
one bar after another.

YEAR BOOK

Everybody knows a John McCullough.
You went to St. Ann's grammar school
with him. He either sat up front
or hid in the back, never said a word
or answered every science and math
question, wore frayed hand me downs
and smelled like he never learned how
to wipe his own ass or wore bright bow ties
and carried a school bag, a colorful lunch box.
Even the nuns shook their heads. Cool
without trying and smart without opening
a book, you carried one spiral notebook
tied in a rubber strap every day. You played
point guard and pitched on school teams,
started drinking when you were eleven
and both Theresa DiPalma and Geraldine Quinn
let you play with their big tits as long
as you promised not to tell anyone.
You never did anything bad to McCullough.
Sometimes you felt sorry for him, thought
of stopping and talking when you saw him
outside of school. But he was such a dick,
the way he lied about his father knowing
Mickey Mantle, bragged about perfect
report cards and how he would volunteer
to sing God Bless America for school assemblies
then roar it out like he was an opera singer.
Somehow you thought he deserved
all the names he was called, every slap
to the back of his head, each time
he was de-pantsed in front of a group
of giggling girls and how on year book
picture day the lunch monitor poured
two pints of chocolate milk over his head.

I met John again at the end of college.
He was the co-editor of a respected journal
and he had accepted two of my first
poems. He invited me over his house,
introduced me to the staff—three
attractive, literary looking, girls
that I didn't think I had a chance to get
even though they kept touching my arm
and smiling and telling me they'd like
to read more of my work—as someone
he knew years ago. There was wine,
cheese, and galleys for the next issue
were scattered on the dining room table.
We didn't say anything meaningful
to or about each other. Later, he put
on some classical music, asked me
if I played ping-pong. Not in a long time,
but I thought anything would be better
than talking poetry and listening
to that crap. John beat me 15-2.
He teased me with lobs and trick shots,
smashed the ball past my helpless
swings. His smiling moon face beamed
as he announced play by play in a nasal
Marv Albert voice, color commented
on how good I used to be at everything,
how I would never have believed
that he, John McCullough, could beat me,
be better than me in anything.
He was right. When he asked to play
it back, I wanted to smash the paddle
across his face. John fucking McCullough.
God damn piece of shit editor.

1987

I visit, maybe, once a month.
We still sit at opposite ends
of the table. Ice cracks
as warm soda pours, scrambles
cubes. We pass pot roast, mashed
potatoes, salt and pepper. Knives
scratch against forks, lips
smack. You think the Yankees
need more pitching. For once,
you might be right. Guidry
is getting old and Righetti
keeps letting late inning leads
disappear. You ask about work,
wonder when my next raise is due.

Mom says there's plenty, goes
into the kitchen to refill
the serving dishes. You change
chairs, move closer to me. Elbows
on the table, one hand plays
with scattered crumbs. The other
picks up a napkin, squeezes it
into a small tight ball. Your throw
hits the kitchen wall, misses
the pail and falls to the floor.
You stop me from getting it, say
"They're cutting back at work again.
This time it could be me. I'm fifty-two.
What the hell am I supposed to do?"

PHYSICS

This morning, the narrator
of the book I'm reading
is trying to fall asleep listening
to a tape on physics. A crisp
scientific voice is explaining
there's no such thing as the past,
that each moment exists forever
caught in a stringy tangle of light
and mass, and I remember
this woman I hardly knew
telling me she lost her virginity
and finalized her third divorce
the same date the atom bomb,
code named "Little Boy,"
was dropped on Hiroshima
killing more than 155,000 people.
August sixth, 1945. Louis Armstrong
died that day in 1971 and in 1948
a freak heat wave off the coast
of Central Portugal pushed
temperatures up to 158° for two
minutes. Wouldn't It Be Nice
was a top ten hit that week
in 1966, the summer I kissed
a girl and felt my first t-shirt
covered tit playing 'Seven Minutes
In Heaven' with Geraldine Quinn
while our friends counted down.

I thought about a Saturday
in that same summer. My team
beats St. Kevin's rich kids, wins
the 8th Grade, CYO championship.
The girl I like sits in the stands,
her hair wrapped high in curlers
as I strike out the last guy
with an inside fastball. I punch
my fist in my mitt, hug
John Calamari my catcher
and roll on the ground
with everybody else in a jumble
of joy. I'm sitting on
the bench, untying my spikes
and my dad leans down,
"Three for four and a one-hitter,
that's what you're supposed
to do, all damn time." He smiles,
slaps the bill of my hat.

Later, at around 7:15 or so
I realize it's the anniversary
of the day my father died.
I call my mom and both
of us find it hard to believe
eight years have already passed.
Always, I want Mickey Mantle
to be chasing down fly balls
in Yankee Stadium, Jeter
making that back hand flip
against Oakland over and over.

Somehow, it's always the night
after Christmas. Snow falls
in fat sexy flakes. Suzanne
walks over, sits on my couch
and plays with her scarf, says
she doesn't know why she's here,
she really loves her boyfriend.
I've never done anything
like this before either. Usually,
I'm slow and awkward,
but I start kissing her
like I know what I'm doing
and she kisses me back softer
and deeper and walks through
the kitchen and into my bedroom
then comes back the next night
and both of us start to fall in love.

And tonight, when I turn out
the lights and pile the covers
high around my head, I wish
that physicist was singing me
to sleep, a sweet rhyming lullaby
in angelic Brian Wilson harmony,
telling me all about another
woman I love, her son's
big green, owl-shaped clock
sitting on his dresser and how
he keeps it set to the same time
no matter how many nights
I sneak in while he's sleeping

to move its wings. It's 3:12
again. His mom has his arms
and I have a hold of his legs.
We're swinging Joshua, higher
and higher until he nearly
scrapes the ceiling. We let go
and he is flying, suspended over
his big soft bed and laughing.

WHEN I GROW UP

The first thing I wanted to be
was a fire truck: shiny, red
careening down busy streets
my arms a long ladder climbing
tenements and reaching a boy
screaming out a smoky window.
Then, like every other boy,
I dreamed of being Number 7
Mickey Mantle flying around
the bases with a slight limp.
Later, I wanted to play bass
for the Young Rascals, standing
stage left next to Felix, head
down, eyes hiding behind bangs,
singing scratchy harmonies,
plucking blue eyed soul
for seriously groovin' white chicks,
or maybe become a free form
late night DJ tagged Joe,
Just The Facts, Friday
because all I ever said
in a deep dark dive bar voice
was title, artist, year
before spinning the next song.

And tonight, all I want is you
to hop the Fort Hamilton
turnstiles, rush through
just closing F train doors
and ride all the way to Queens,
walk those three quiet blocks,
cut across the park and knock

while I stand in the foyer
ten, twenty seconds wondering
if I should yell, tell you
to go fuck yourself or slowly
open my arms so you can sink
into me like you made it home
to where you always belonged.

BOY SCOUTS

Kevin went from tent
to tent. He waved a pocket
flashlight back and forth,
untied the flap and pushed

his head through the opening.
"Anybody for a blow job, only
twenty-five cents?" Joey,
my best friend, unzipped

his sleeping bag, flipped him two bits.
I turned over, kept my back to them
and tried not to listen:
gentle kissing sounds, fast

uneven breathing. I felt my eyes start
to cry and my cock get hard.

SWEET SIXTEEN

He walks in
without ringing
the bell. Stringy
hair hides his eyes,
two gold studs pierce
each ear, a torn
tee shirt shows off
tattoos. He leans
against the banister,
shifts his weight
boot to boot
as he waits
for my little sister.

I watch him, think
about the time Mom
and Dad wouldn't stop
fighting and we climbed
down the fire escape
and she hopped on
the back of my bike's
soft banana seat,
wrapped her arms
around my waist
as we raced down
hill and she held
on even tighter.

She walks downstairs:
shiny black boots,
a tight skirt, white
tank top. She kisses

his cheek and they both
laugh. They walk out
holding hands, brushing
shoulders. She climbs
into his jeep. He leans
over, kisses her lips
as his hand fits
between her smooth
baby fat thighs.

KISSING

It still embarrasses me
any time I think about
Tommy Dunn and 7th grade,
that party he took me aside
and tried to explain how to kiss
with not too wet lips pressed
softly, slightly open, moving
slowly and never sucking
like a fucking vacuum cleaner.
I probably nodded, quickly moved
to another part of the basement
before he brought up tongues
and what I was supposed to do
with mine while everyone thought
we were homos or something nearly
as awful. But no, I was just slow—
I still liked baseball cards and snow
balls better than girls—and scared.
I kept glancing over at Regina,
Geraldine and Claire sitting
against the wall, whispering
behind their hands, looking
at me and laughing. For years,
I would jerk off taking turns
picturing one of them walking
across the room, taking my hand,
leading me to an upstairs bedroom
and teaching me everything.

I thought of Dunn a couple
of years ago. An ex-girlfriend
was flying into the city visiting

her sick parents every chance
she could and spending as many
hours in my bed as possible.
We kissed and kissed until
we fell back in love, whispered
about her filing for divorce.
At the same time, an unhappy
woman half my age was calling
a few times a day, knocking
on my door and sneaking away
three or four times a week
from a boyfriend too busy
and bored to kiss and touch her
like I did. She kept telling me
I was handsome, saying
she was completely in love
with me and how she wanted
to leave Bill. I imagined Dunn
was living somewhere in Texas,
working in finance with thinning
red hair and a roly-poly build.
He was on his second marriage
and couldn't stop worrying
about his sad, quiet kids.
I wanted to sit on a stoop
in Queens with him, talk
about the few things I learned
and somehow found myself
believing in, why I still wished
Suzanne and Erica missed
kissing me and what the hell
he thought was wrong with me.

VIGILS

I hug my mother, try to put
a twenty into her hand,
convince her to take a taxi
home. I feed him a few
spoonfuls of cherry jello,
hold the cup as he sucks
a bent straw. We both feel
better when he falls asleep.
We love each other, but ran
out of things to say last
Monday. We stopped talking
about the time I was five
riding on his shoulders
as he carried me up
the ramp for my first look
at the Yankee Stadium infield
as green and magical as Gates
to Emerald City; or at nineteen
when he changed his seat
at the dinner table, told
my mother he couldn't keep
his food down while looking
at me and my friggin' long hair.
I kept staring into my plate,
ate faster. I must have sighed
or raised my eyes to the ceiling
because he charged around the table,
grabbed the back of my hair,
yanked on it and held me there,
balanced on the back legs
of the chair, daring me to make
one more friggin' sound

as my mother kept yelling
his name, yelling to let me go.

Instead, I watch Seinfeld
re-running on the monitor
hanging over his head,
try to anticipate the lines
that always make me laugh.
Later, I sit by the window,
stare at the buildings lighting
up, kitchen after kitchen.
I nod to the daughter
of the man in the next bed
as she walks in. He's dying
too. I watch her ass, wish
this was a movie. We'd go
for dinner, linger over
coffee in a nearby café,
hold hands while we wait
for a light to change, end up
in her cramped apartment.
But no, there's nothing to say
or do. Our fathers are racing
in slow motion toward whatever
comes next or nothing
at all. Neither of us sure
if the winner is the one
who fights to stay alive,
or lets go, dies tonight.

ARRANGEMENTS

I sit at the head
of the table now.
The funeral director
opens his book, shows
pictures of caskets,
flower arrangements, quotes
prices. I turn pages, point,
nod. My mother chooses
a wool suit for him
to wear. "His favorite,"
my sister says twice.
It's navy blue,
like my catholic school
uniform. I remember
that first Monday morning
how he wiped a clear space
in the steamed-up mirror,
crouched behind me, knotted
my tie and splashed a bit
of Old Spice on my face.
There will be two days
to view the body
at Duden's funeral home
back in Brooklyn. Last Christmas,
I drove him to Midnight Mass.
When he asked me to come
inside, I coughed, said, "Dad,
you know I stopped believing
years ago." He grabbed
the door handle, answered,
"Not even tonight?"
I played with the radio knobs,

told him I'd be out front
by one. I drove halfway
down the block, stopped
and watched in the rear view
mirror, the way he gripped
the railing as he climbed
the steps carefully, paused
at the door and tried
to catch his breath.
Mass will be at St. Lucy's,
ten o'clock, Tuesday morning.
Father Eugene will lead the service
and I will read the eulogy.

CROSSING

Larry turned eighteen
in May. He knows
what red and green mean,
walks to the corner
and looks both ways.
Today, he's on his own
for the first time.
He walks out the door.
I count to thirty, follow.
Hidden behind the stoop,
I watch him. Head down,
hands deep in pockets,
he drags his feet,
twirls on one foot
every twenty steps,
then bends and pulls up
his socks. He turns
the corner. I run down
the block, duck behind
a black Cadillac.
When he reaches the curb,
I sneak closer, crouch
in the hardware store's
doorway. Larry lifts
his head, sees a red
light. His lips quiver,
right hand karate chops
his open left palm.
I recognize the sign
for stop, whisper
"Good." Larry looks up
and the light's green.

His right fist winds
around his clenched left
hand, tells him to walk.
He checks for cars, half
runs across Bergen Street.
Safe, Larry pirouettes
and faces me. He bows
at the waist, straightens
up, yells "Okay Tony"
and laughs out loud.

DISNEY WORLD

John's the highest functioning guy
in the group home. He always
says hello, asks about your day,
smiles and never forgets your name
like I often will. Everybody
loves him and every Monday
he sits by my desk, tells me
about his wonderful weekend
whether he went to the movies
Friday night, spent Saturday
winning medals and ribbons
at Special Olympics, played
Coney Island Skee Ball
all Sunday afternoon or sat
on the couch staring into space
with Channel 13's pledge week
blaring in the background.

No, he's not on any medication
and no I'm not too jealous
he appears happier than me.
Maybe I should be grateful
he doesn't shit or piss his pants,
rip his shirts or throw chairs
at the ceiling like the others
and be satisfied helping him
learn to cook, cross streets,
count his money. Yet sometimes
he pisses me off with the way
he says he likes everything
exactly the same amount
and never lets anyone know

44

what he's thinking or feeling,
how he takes so long to answer
a question or make a simple
choice as if he's worried
or scared that anything he says
will be wrong and something
terrible will happen to him
and sometimes, I admit it,
I do imagine smacking
that sweet dumb boring smile
right off his damn mouth.

But I've tried to let John know
that this life is his and my job
is to help him live it the way
he likes, that it's okay to tell me
what he wants and doesn't want
and he doesn't need permission
to feel sad or bad or angry.
Every once in a while I think
he's beginning to understand.
I now know he'd rather eat
McDonald's than Chinese food,
that there's no way he'll ever
get on a roller coaster or step
into a pool more than two feet
deep while wearing a life jacket
and holding a staff member's hand,
that he prefers staying home
watching Country Music Awards
over sitting in tenth row seats

as Springsteen and the E Streeters
play a benefit show. I tell myself,
it's okay, everyone has opinions
and fears, none are good or bad
and I try to pretend to believe
that bull shit when talking to John.

Still, these past few days,
John's really surprised me.
I didn't know what to say
when he told me he'd rather not
let me borrow a Johnny Cash CD
I gave him for his last birthday.
Even though I swore I'd buy him
a new one if I broke or lost it,
he shook his head no, said
if it was okay with me, he wanted
to keep the one he had. Today
when he asked about my day,
I told him I was tired and stressed
worrying about his roommate.
John hoped Rob would get well,
come home from the hospital soon.
He then paused for a moment
asked if this meant that he, John,
wouldn't be going to Disney World.
I tried to describe what it meant
to be generous and thoughtful, why
no one really likes self serving
cheap bastards. When he looked
down, took a deep breath, I thought

he might apologize. Instead, John
asked about Florida again, started
clapping when I finished explaining
about reservations, penalty fees
and packing properly for an 8:00 AM
flight out of LaGaurdia next Monday.

BATH TIME

His right hand
grips the safety rail.
My right hand fits
under his arm pit,
helps him step
into the tub, sit
down. His eyes shut,
lips form a tight kiss
as his ass hits
hot water. He wets
the wash cloth, reaches
in the soap dish,
lets the soap slip
through his grasp, slide
down by his feet.
He bends over,
bumps his head
on the faucet,
slurs, "Shhtt." I stop
myself from laughing,
fish for the soap,
lather up the rag,
scrub his hunched
back, bony shoulders.
I give him the wash cloth.
"Start with your arms Rob."
He rubs up and down,
moves to his neck,
chest, legs. "Don't
forget your face."
He pats his cheeks,
his chin. I grab the rag,

tell him, "Shut your eyes
tight," and wash his face.
Soap still gets in,
stings. One hand balls
into a fist, rubs
his eyes. The other
slaps the water. I get
a towel, dry his face,
say, "Stop acting
like a damn baby."
He blinks open his eyes,
mumbles, "Sorry Townry."
I muss up his hair,
"No problem, my bad,"
and point to his penis.
He strokes small circles.
We both watch it
harden, rise above
soapy water. I draw
the shower curtain,
sit on the closed
toilet lid, light
a cigarette.
                Finished,
Robert's hand rattles
the plastic curtain. I stand,
slide it open. His eyes
stare straight ahead.
I hold the tube of shampoo,
watch the green gel
squeeze into my palm,
become white foam

49

as my fingers spread it
through his hair. I turn
on the shower, test
the temperature, aim
the hand held nozzle,
rinse his body clean.
Water swirls down
the drain. I help him
get up, step out
of the tub. I open
a bath towel, wrap it
around his waist.
He places his hands
on my shoulders. Heat
rises off his skin, fills
the space between us.

A GOOD BAD DAY

John walks slowly up the stairs
to my office every day. Between
four and four-thirty, after the bus
brings him home from day program
and after he uses the bathroom,
he says, "Oh, hello Tony," as if
he's surprised to find me
sitting at my desk. He says
he had a good day, stands
by a chair and after six years
of living at the residence,
his home, he still hesitates,
wonders if he needs permission
to sit down. I don't give it,
wait until he sits on his own.
He tells me if he read or colored,
exercised or sang today and I ask
questions as if I was his mother.
Maybe he went to a park, a store,
the library. All along he wears
this pleasant, half smiling,
perfectly balanced, zen-like gaze
across his Fred Flintstone face.
And I don't know if I'm stressed
or bored, mean or just a smart-ass
acting like we are friends;
but when he asks me about my day
sometimes I tell him the truth.

Uselessly endless meetings, piles
of paper work, asshole administrators.
Not enough sleep. Girlfriend trouble.

Yesterday, I told him that a woman
I loved is getting married on a boat
in September and I wished
I owned a torpedo. He didn't say
anything, just sat there smiling
and I'm sorry, but I couldn't help it,
I had to ask him if he ever
had a bad day. When he said no,
none that he could remember,
I said are you sure. He said
I don't think so and looked like
he was thinking hard. I leaned
forward, said that I felt very sad
when my father died and I wondered
how he felt when his mom and dad
passed away. John jutted out his chin,
looked beyond me and said yeah
that was a bad day. When I asked
if he missed them, he chewed
on his lips, said sometimes.
I said I know what you mean.

4/17/06

A day like this
and I can almost consider
believing in God.
It's early afternoon
in an April that refuses
to show any hint of Spring.
I take off from work
to spend all day in bed
with someone who loves me.
Her black slip is bunched
above her waist and my cock
is poking through my boxers
when the bell rings. Don't
worry, it's not her boyfriend
catching us again. Just pizza
arriving a bit too quickly.
I can hear her laughing
as I try to hide my hard-on
underneath an oversized
Jets jersey while I search
for my wallet and make
small talk with the guy
at the door. She makes fun
of my plastic utensils.
I laugh at how she strips
the layers of cheese off
before she takes a bite.

We keep touching
each other as we eat
six slices in record time
and race back to bed.

Leaning majestically against
two propped up pillows,
God watches our fingers
and tongues do what they were
made for and God nods
when I push inside her, start
to move. God knows
no one has said anything
truer when I whisper
nothing has ever felt
this good and she answers,
"Not since last Thursday."

After, when she presses
her head against my chest,
tangles her legs in mine
and nearly drifts off
to sleep, God, that wise-ass,
is smiling with a perfect
combination of innocence
and skepticism. God knows
how badly I want to believe
she will leave that damn Bill.
I lie, promise to go to church
every Sunday, eat his body
and drink his blood if my prayer
is answered. We both glance
at the table-top alarm clock
and I shrug. I know, I know,
there are boyfriends and
terrorists all over the world

and if everything goes
perfectly, we have another
one hour and forty-five minutes
to love and fuck some more.

MY OTHER LIFE

I live on the outskirts
of some controllable city
in Virginia or Vermont.
Most mornings, I jog two
miles, eat balanced breakfasts,
glance at my watch often.
Gene Hackman reads
a Grisham novel or Kenny G
plays his sax softly
whenever I drive. My cell phone
nestles between my legs
and I'm counting on a big
Christmas bonus, my rumored
promotion come June.
I am, of course, married.
Her name is Harriet May
and she always calls me honey
or darling in a gentle tone.
Her blonde hair is cut short
and she works part time
at the Children's Hospital.

We live in a two story
townhouse with tall windows.
The neighbors are all white
and English is their first
and only language. We wave
to each other across lawns
and bushes, sometimes stop
to plot weekend barbecues.
Jordan and Will, our two boys,
are still young enough to kiss me

without blushing. They want
to be figure skaters, lawyers,
ministers when they grow up.
I make sure they eat vegetables,
brush their teeth before bed.
In another year or two,
I'll buy them guns, teach them
to hunt and shoot responsibly.

In my other life
my father is still alive.
He saw the best specialists
and they found a donor
in time. Insurance covered
the cost and bill collectors never
call during dinner. He and mother
will spend Christmas with us.
They'll say we're spoiling
the children, then tiptoe
into their bedrooms, fill
their piggy banks with tens
and twenties. They'll talk
about Brooklyn, sick and dead
relatives, remember the names
of the four women I swore
I couldn't live without. We'll laugh,
wonder what the hell was I thinking,
filling all those spiral notebooks
like I was some kind of Steinbeck
or Dylan, Springsteen, Carver.

NOT THE WORST THING

At dinner, Don's new girlfriend
talks about the one time she hit
her son. He was five and screaming,
squirming loose of his seat belt harness.
She kept half turning, reaching
behind to strap him back in, begging
him to stop as cars sped by, horns
blared. When she started to pull out,
he grabbed the back of her hair
and yanked. She turned, smacked him
twice. Two years ago and her eyes
show she isn't close to forgiving
herself. Don strokes Sue's hand
with his thumb. She's separated
from her third husband. Each one
sounds more abusive than the one before.
Don stopped speaking to his parents
years before he started to suspect
they did unspeakable things to him.
Somewhere, deep down, he's measuring
those two slaps and what they mean
to his girlfriend, her son, their future.
I dip a chip in the salsa, ask
if her son ever pulled her hair again.

I agree it's not the point, but I'd bet
he hasn't done anything like that again.
Sometimes, a good well-timed smack
across the face isn't the worst thing.
When I say this, they glance at each
other. The waitress brings the check.
I have to hurry, meet my new girlfriend

in fifteen minutes. She's half my age
and we ended up in bed too quickly.
We're learning about each other,
finding out how we fit together
while she lies against my chest
and waits to see if my cock will get
hard again. Last time, she talked
about her white trash Jersey childhood,
the night her next door neighbor called
the cops and her dad was arrested.
Her head had swelled big as a watermelon.
She said it was her fault and she still
feels bad. She kept sticking her face
into her dad's face and asking him
if he felt good beating up a girl,
daring him to try and shut her up
every time he was ready to stop.

I didn't know what to say, shifted
position, leaned on one arm. I touched
her hair, kissed her closed eyes
until she started to kiss me back.
My father hit me four, five times.
I can still feel the weight of his hand,
the sting hitting my skin, flashing
down my spine. I remember trying
not to cry until I made it to my room,
my little brother sitting on his bed,
asking if I was alright and telling him
to leave me the hell alone. Probably
I put on head phones, played the loudest

music I owned and filled my head
with scenes of torturing my father
as he wasted away in a nursing home.
Hours later he would knock on my door
or call me down stairs to talk. I think
we'd apologize, make promises. We might
have hugged, or maybe we didn't touch
at all. Still, I always felt better, almost
closer, as if we had forgiven each other
something terrible because I loved him
and I knew he loved me more than anything.

LOVE AND BASEBALL

The Yankees are down 5 to 2
to the Red Sox with one out
in the eighth inning. It's the seventh
game and Pedro is pitching.
You can turn the light off now,
pull up the blanket and go to sleep.
Or when Tom calls from Philly
asking if the Yanks have a chance,
you can lie and tell him, "Yeah,
they hit the ball hard in the seventh
and Pedro always runs out of gas,"
as Jeter lines a double to right.
Stay on the phone, pretend it's good
luck. Talk about Suzanne. She's half
your age. You've been seeing her
the past eight months. She's smart
and funny, has big tits, full soft
lips, a boyfriend she lives with.
At a bar, Tom would buy beers
until closing, genuflect at your feet,
call you his hero. He'd wear
this silly grin, tell you how lucky
you are. "You mean, she comes over,
you fuck, and she just goes home?"

You'd shrug your shoulders, hold
your hands out to the side,
surprised it's happening to you.
He'd stop listening as you tried
to explain there's much more to it,
that it's better than he could imagine.
Both of you would grow quiet,

remember women who broke
your hearts and, for one dumb
blessed moment, Suzanne makes up
for all of them. On the screen,
Bernie bangs out a hit. Grady Little,
that dumb shit, visits the mound,
sticks with Pedro. You tell Tom
you've fallen in love. You can hear
his stubbled chin rub against
the mouthpiece as he shakes his head.
You tell him she loves you too.
She said the best parts of her life
are the hours talking on the phone,
the times you walk hand in hand
after a movie, rainy weekdays spent
in bed. But the night her boyfriend
found out, she called crying.

Matsui, Posada double, tie the score.
The stadium's speakers blare "Enter
Sandman" as Mariano trots in
from the bull pen. Later, she told you
the difference between being in love
with you and that she still loves Bill.
It means that if he will forgive her,
she will do anything to try and fix
things. They've been together
since she was nineteen, his family
is her family and she's not strong
enough to leave him, live on her own.
It has nothing to do with you.

You were perfect and she's sorry
she can't love you the way you deserve.
And no, it doesn't matter how unhappy
she's been the last two and a half years.
She threw his car keys in the yard,
wrapped her arms around his legs
as he left with a shopping bag of clothes
and now you're trying to forget her.
Yet, any time the phone rings,
you hope it's Suzanne. She's with him
and you feel sad and empty, foolish, old.

Meanwhile, Mariano throws three
scoreless innings, the Red Sox bring
Wakefield in and she still sometimes
calls. She sends gifts, deep soft pillows
for your bed, slips a burned CD
under your door when you're not home.
You're playing it the next time she calls
to tell you about a dream she had: you,
her, the softball field near her house
and a little boy. She was pitching
a wiffle ball underhanded. You were
helping the kid hold the bat, swing.
Sometimes, little boys grow up
to become Aaron Boone, they hit
a fluttering knuckleball over
the wall and into the night
and the Yankees win the pennant,
the Yankees win the pennant.
Sometimes, you walk off the field

with your head down and end up
alone, your sleep restless, troubled.
You spend your life missing
something you got so close to,
the thing you think you wanted most.

NUMBER 32

Today I am taking the A Train
away from Duke Ellington's
Harlem and into East New York
Brooklyn. This beautiful tall blonde
and I are the only two Caucasians
in the crowded car. With each stop,
we move closer, pulled
together by some unnamed force.
We both know not to look
at anyone too long and even
when I make eye contact
with her, I pause for less
than a second before rushing
to read advertisements for laser
surgery. I am not scared,
not worried, just incredibly aware
of how white, like a bleached
sheet drying on a line, I feel.
I want to lean closer, whisper
in a cool, irresistible way
for her to come to my place
so we can hurry up and start
making some more of us.
When the train eases into
the next station, the doors slide
open and this young, buffed,
light skin, black man, struts
onto the train wearing
a Buffalo Bills number 32
Simpson jersey, and I want
to know what it means

to him and everyone else.
Is it sweep right, OJ gliding
behind Reggie McKenzie,
piling up 2000 yards? OJ
hurtling suitcases in crowded
airports for Hertz, guest
starring on The Love Boat?

This guy in the jersey must
remember that slow motion
car chase interrupting the Knicks
playoff game? OJ's murdered
white ex-wife and the white guy
who drove her home? Johnny
Cocharan? Me, I was working
at the group home, the only
white person on the payroll
with people I still call friends
when the not guilty verdict
was announced. I watched
Jean fall to her knees, thank
Jesus as her arms reached
for the ceiling. Annette twirled
in a circle clapping so hard
that sparks of sweat shot out.
The two men shook hands.
I wasn't quite sure why
but I realized it was a time
when we couldn't say anything
to each other. I walked outside,
sat on the stoop and waited

for yellow buses to bring
our boys back from school.
Back on the subway, that guy
is talking to the woman, jotting
numbers on a scrap of paper
and she's smiling, touching
her pretty blonde hair, folding
the paper in her jacket pocket.
Maybe she will call him tomorrow,
they can go for drinks or dinner
or dancing. Maybe they will fall
in love, spend their honeymoon
searching for the real killers.

SOFTBALL

I throw my spikes and glove
in the back seat. We nod
hello, swap late night scores.
The radio twangs country.
I open the window, hang
my head out and hope
he drives fast enough to blow
that noise away. I don't ask
about the money he owes me.
He doesn't care why I left
my last girlfriend. No one
will bring up the dismissal
of his latest DUI or his poor
health and he's never read
anything I've written.

The sun hurts my eyes
as we fly by lines of cars.
He's five years younger
and since our Father died
I'm the one mom will call
with the news of John's next
car accident, his second heart
attack. I don't know what
I'll say to my Mother, how
I'll explain I could never
help my brother. I wish
I was still twelve years old
and we were play fighting
before bedtime, laughing
and rolling on the floor
and I knew I could pin him
make him do anything.

We trot across the outfield
grass, warm up by the dugout.
The ball whips back and forth,
cracks leather. I pitch, bat
third. He hits clean up, plays
first base. I bounce a single
up the middle. He lines one
to right. I round second, dig
for third knowing I'm too old
for this shit. The coach yells,
"Down. Down." I go in head first,
just beat the tag slapping the back
of my neck. My brother eases
into second, clapping. I lie
on the ground, hugging the bag.

BLACK AND WHITE

I sometimes took the F train
home from work with Lois
and could feel her cringe
anytime a smelly black beggar
stepped in front of us, held
out his hand and god blessed us
even when we never gave them
a penny. She'd shake her head
and her black face would grimace
anytime a gaggle of teenagers
took over our car; the girls
clacking gum, swinging their fat
ghetto earrings and the boys
swaggering around in those baggy,
low riding jeans and showing off
their funky ass underwear, saying
fuck this and nigger that. She'd lean
over, grab my forearm and whisper
how she'd like to take a switch
to every one of their mothers
while wishing she had the guts
to tell them to stop acting
the fool and disgracing her.

Mondays, we'd talk about weekends.
Hers were a visiting nurse job,
a long hot bath, candles, wine,
some long time lover she'd toss
out before she left for church.
Mine was a movie or concert,
an old girlfriend back in town,
dinner with a new woman, hardly

better than being alone writing.
Sundays, I'd sometimes visit
my mom and someone, my brother,
my sister or my cousin the cop
would slip in the word nigger
somewhere between the pasta and meat
about some spoiled selfish athlete,
our ruined old Brooklyn neighborhood
or welfare and Sharpton and fatherless
children and I'd keep eating, never
saying a word except to please pass
the lasagna, knowing I couldn't
change anybody's mind and trying
to believe that nothing they said
had anything to do with me.

YANKEE STADIUM MATINEE 2008

You've cut work and feel free,
giddy like the time you played
hooky from sixth grade and found
a bundle of tied together Playboys
dumped in the Kissena Park lots.
Your breath quickens and legs
tire as you climb to your cheap,
nose bleeder seats. But you're perched
behind home plate and can still tell
a fastball from a curve, still catch
the first step every fielder
will take when bat meets ball.
After standing for the anthem,
scanning the crowd hopefully
for half naked, nearby women,
it's the throw down to second,
the ball tossed around the horn
and the Yanks versus Padres,
two underachieving teams
looking to start a hot streak.
Tim gets two hot dogs, a beer
poured from a dark blue bottle
as you unwrap the fat Italian hero
you bought from a nearby deli
named after Joltin' Joe Di Maggio.

The game begins and you talk:
playoff possibilities, 'to DH or not
to DH,' whether Joba should start
or relieve, how badly you'll miss
this magical old Stadium when greed
tears it down at season's end.

Giles leads off with a double
down the line and someone says
'there goes the no hitter.'
Your friend's never seen one.
You watched Jim Bunning pitch
his perfect game against
the Mets, Father's Day 1964.
You were ten years old, bored,
fidgety and hoping for a slugfest.
Today, you'd give anything to sit
next to your dad in the middle
of a pitching duel and remember
all those twilights playing catch
with him, shagging flies, getting
in front of grounders, the sounds
of the ball whipping back and forth,
smacking leather, trying to say things
you never learned to tell each other.

The Yanks are winning 2-1
and you're hoping they can hand
the ball to Riviera with a lead
as the crowd starts the dreaded wave.
Tim asks about your writing.
It's going slow. Sometimes you worry
you're writing the same damn crap
over and over. You mention a recent
acceptance from a tiny journal
no one will ever read, sending out
your new manuscript and all
the rejections. You'll spend next

weekend with an ex-girlfriend
and her son who you still love.
Joshua's turning fourteen.
He's autistic and gradually
growing further out of control.
Tim describes his writing as steady
and smooth. His book's still selling
well and he's happy, completely
in love with a woman whose name
you repeatedly mispronounce.
They're spending autumn in France,
thinking of renting a house
on the Cape. He can't believe
such good fortune has found him
so late in his life. You know Tim,
his hard work, his heartache
and you try not to think why him
and not you. You're younger, maybe
better looking, maybe a better writer.
You're not even hoping he'll help you
with publications, university readings
at least not yet. And as Mariano
steps through the bull pen gate
all you feel is good, good for him.
You think Tim deserves all this
and more, nearly as much as you do,
as you picture hurling him off
the top tier, his body lying twisted
and lifeless on the dugout steps.

MID LIFE POETRY CRISIS

Sometimes I get sick
of seeing myself
in my poems, my Brooklyn
accent slurring its way
through every line,
whining about settling
into middle age, mostly
on my own, sometimes
lonely, while mulling over
every thing that's missing.

I'm tired of song titles,
retards, autistic kids,
old and new girlfriends,
battered valentines, baseball
metaphors, not getting
laid, subway stations,
working class families,
drunk drivers, dead fathers
and every one else who never
try to talk to each other.

I want to open a window,
walk down a fire escape
without waking anyone,
without leaving a note. Walk
into a bank of coastal fog
and disappear. Come out
on the other side, thirty
years younger, go back
to school, get an MFA.

I want to believe in God,
language poetry, the power
of rhyme. Become witty,
clever and vague, cutting,
but sensitive and politically
correct. Wear a frayed
blazer, shave my balls,
smoke cigarettes, get
an ancient Japanese symbol
tattooed to my bicep, stand
around sipping cocktails.

I want to write poems
filled with abstract meaning,
Greek Goddesses, second
generation immigrants
searching for identity,
down to earth lesbians,
World Trade Center
heroes, villains, victims,
all their greedy relatives.

I want to write a sonnet
about a thin woman
viewing a Matisse print
from thirteen different
angles. Write a haiku,
put a bumblebee in it,
the sound its wings make
brushing a fucking tulip.

I want to open my mail
to submission requests
from the New Yorker
and Poetry. Act humble
when nominations, awards
roll in. Put my agent
on hold. Teach at summer
conferences. Sell more books
than Billy Collins and Jewel
combined. And when I die,
bored, tortured school kids
will be forced to recite
my poems during
National Poetry Month.

GOOD

After a week of rain, it's sunny and May.
It's spring, you're walking Brooklyn streets
and you got this inkling that something good
could be beginning when you step to the side,
let a young mother wheel her stroller slowly by
and her smile reminds you of Diane. Ah Diane,
that years-ago girl with her shiny black skin
and wise-ass mouth, the tiny sound she made
the first time you undid the two top buttons
of her jeans, hooked your finger inside her
as you stood on the Bergen Street station
waiting for the F train to come. The way
she rocked herself to sleep the five weeks
you couldn't keep your hands off each other,
even after she told you that first morning
she was pregnant, maybe two months along.
You said you never would have guessed
and she said her breasts already felt bigger
and fuller and you kissed and sucked them
until you started fucking again. She never
mentioned the father and looked at you
like you were crazy when you asked about
an abortion. Somehow, she had it in her head
she was carrying a girl and named her Sydney.
She said she didn't give a shit if she turned
into a fat ass project mama like her mother.

It wasn't too long before she started wondering
what was going on with you. You didn't know,
said you needed time while she kept coming over.
You tried convincing yourself you were in love,
pictured growing old together. She ended it

78

one Monday morning, saying it would never work.
You mumbled something about bad timing, how
much you would miss her. Mostly, you remember
trying to stop yourself from thinking you'd give
almost anything to fuck her one more time.
She got out of bed, showered real quick and fit
her things into a red back pack while you threw on
sweat pants, wishing she was the kind of woman
you usually fell for, the kind who lived according
to some plan, the kind who believed abortion
was a right and a sacrament, the nice white kind.
When she wouldn't let you walk her to the subway,
you kissed her cheek at the door. You're pretty sure
you called a few times, left messages with cousins
as you counted down the months, feeling better
and better until you knew she was gone for good.

ON OR OFF

The Yanks are done for the year
and I've run out of things
to talk about while Moses
waits for me to decide
if I want a poppy
or sesame bagel
every morning, wait
for him to scramble
eggs, brown the sausage.

He's trying to make eye
contact and I suspect
it will be a cold, silent
uncomfortably long time
until pitchers and catchers
if I don't say something
soon, so I blurt out,
confess, brag, I nailed
this new chick last night
and his brown, possibly
tortured, immigrant eyes
double or triple in size.

I go on, tell him that
when it was time to fall
into bed, she asked, "Boots,
on or off." Finally, he says
something in Spanish,
something especially dirty
I'm sure, ending with one
reverent, hushed, drawn out
hopeful, English word,

"Boots?" And when I nod,
he leaps across the counter,
gives me a loud high five
and yells, "Fuck yeah, bro."

I smile, look to see
if any other customers
are watching and let him
believe what he wants to.
I don't say I didn't hear
or understand the question,
that she had to ask me again
or that it didn't matter to me,
that I didn't even help slide
her boots off. I just watched.

I pay my four dollars
and twenty-five cents,
tell Moses to take it easy
and don't mention that all
I wanted was to hold her
tight, get inside her, stay
until late morning, look
in her eyes as I left, see
she was already missing
me, my hands and mouth
all over her, sweet, soft, slow
and hard, thinking about
the next time. Soon.

Maybe then I'll think
about boots, thigh high,

shiny, black, buckles
and heels, garters, fish
nets, whips and chains,
countertops, two AM subway
stations, back seat taxis,
crusty fire escapes. Maybe
some day, one day, please,
she'll suggest adding a friend.
How about a silky Asian,
a suicidal MFA student,
art therapists and guidance
counselors, sixteen year old
Latinas, my cousin Patricia
who still lives in Bensonhurst,
twin down syndrome sisters,
full-titted retro hippie maidens
from Vermont? But no, not
too fat and no, no guys.
No, not even Moses.

HALLOWEEN ON THE F TRAIN

I'm trying to read my book
when Little Red Riding Hood
and the Big Bad Wolf take
the seats across from me.
I can't keep my eyes off
her red low cut blouse,
red fish net stockings,
the goodies in her basket.
The wolf tugs on his mask,
lifts a beer to his snout,
takes a swig and a bit spills
down his chinny chin chin.

I haven't dressed up since
I was eleven, a pirate or Robin
Hood, going door to door filling
a shopping bag with candy,
throwing eggs at kids and cars.
Last year I was with a woman
who loved Halloween. One time
Drena and her best friend stood
on an uptown corner dressed
as good fairies and blessed
passersby with wands, granting
wishes. Part of me was wishing
I could step into a phone booth,
rip off my clothes, slip out
of my skin, drink and dance
and laugh at an all night party,
throw her over the kitchen
table, fuck her until it hurt
or somehow turn into a guy

she'd want to marry, settle
down and have a kid with
before she turned forty
and had to follow her plan
to do it all on her own.

The wolf grumbles. His mask
keeps shifting, chafing his cheeks
and beer dribbles down his neck.
He whines about how long
they spent getting dressed
and maybe if the party sucks
they can stay home next year.
Red adjusts his snout, kisses,
licks his black nostrils, places
her hand on the wolf's leg,
grazes her long red nails near
his crotch as the wolf purrs.

I don't know why Drena cried
twice the night we ended it.
Once, before we fucked, once
after. We never fit that well,
never fell all the way in love.
I kept as quiet as possible
and left before the sun
came up. She sat on the bed
as I pulled my knapsack straps
snug, leaned over, kissed her
neck and stroked her hair
hoping she'd open her robe,

pull me back in. She later wrote
she didn't regret a second
we spent together. I didn't
either, but I didn't tell her
I never spent so much time,
seven months, with someone
that added up to so little.
I once called it a string
of good one night stands
and a friend of mine wondered
what was wrong with that.

Red gives out goodies to kids,
the wolf growls at adults
while I wish the wolf would huff
and puff, blow Red's blouse down
and her full young promising tits
would keep me from imagining
what Drena's wearing tonight,
help me forget how much I miss
watching her undress, stop me
from wondering why we never
could make each other happy
for more than a weekend.

HAPPY

Early Saturday night
and your phone rings.
Maybe it's Nancy, asking
can she catch a cab,
come over? Can we try
again? No, it's Doug.
He worked on two new poems
this morning and he thinks
they're almost there. Mid day
he subwayed to the Bronx,
shot a round of golf. He said
he was happy: the sun,
the grass, the little white ball
rolling into holes. He felt good
going home to read Gatsby,
glad he wasn't the guy sitting
across the train, looking
at his watch, straining
to catch his reflection
in the window. That guy
can't be late. He's meeting
the woman he loves
at seven thirty sharp
and he wants the part
in his hair to be perfect.
You're not sure Doug's
lying anymore. He sounds
convinced he's better off
alone. Most nights, you're
lonely too, trying hard
to believe the same thing.

Today you ate a late lunch
at a diner: bowls of cole
slaw, pickles, lean pastrami.
Outside, the day was setting
records for warmth in February.
Everybody was walking in twos,
holding hands and stepping
into stores like they were boarding
some ark. Your waitress wiped
a countertop. She looked nearly
as old and as tired as you felt
and when the crowd thinned out,
she sat down. You both hated
the song playing on the radio.
She kept tipping the salt shaker,
moving her hands as she talked
about her six year old son.
She said she went to St. Ann's
with your sister, her brother Danny
played little league with you.
You apologized for not remembering,
told her about the group home
you run in Brooklyn, that you want
to be a baseball player, a rock star
or a writer when you grow up.
When you asked if she'd mind
if you came by at the end
of her shift, she took one
of your cold french fries,
put it in her mouth, said ten,
ten thirty would be good.

THOUGHTS AND THEORIES OF SPACE AND DISTANCE WHEN YOUR GIRLFRIEND SAYS SHE WANTS TO LIVE TOGETHER AND YOU SAY YES, MAYBE IN THE SUMMER

You think there's some kind of formula
involving miles per hour and car lengths
one needs to keep between your jeep
and the gray mini van full of kids
making faces out the tinted back window
that equals safety in case of sudden stops.
But you don't know. You don't drive and never
could figure out what X equaled in school.

Five days a week, you stand on a platform
with people who glance at watches, lean
over tracks and look into the dark tunnel,
hoping. You think they should be careful,
stay behind the yellow line. Last night, a man
jumped or fell in front of the train you were on.
You felt the lurch and watched mouths gasping
and screaming, hands dropping packages,
oranges rolling on the ground. Everyone
had to turn away. One woman crumpled
slow motion into a crouch, fell against
a pole. The cops and EMS workers arrived
quicker than seemed possible. Still, the news
led with a decapitated, unidentified man.

Today, when your train comes, you find
a prime standing spot and test your friend's
theory that every rush hour subway car
carries at least one woman you could love
for a long time. No, it's not the blonde
stunning everyone as she saunters off
at Lexington. Not the one with the tiger

tattoo and blow job lips, not even
the pretty one who keeps looking at you
as if your fly's open. It could be the one
reading a book, wearing head phones
and mouthing words with her eyes shut.
From here, it looks like she's reading
The Grapes Of Wrath. Under her breath
she's singing the song you first made love to,
every moan and grunt in perfect pitch.

The woman you love lives three states
away. Every weekend when the pilot
clicks off the seat belt sign, you reach
into the overhead bin and this goofy-ass,
born again grin begins to spread
across your lips and you wind up
hugging and kissing like freed hostages
and you almost forget you're forty-three
fucking years old, that this kind of thing
embarrassed you even when you were young.
You hurry to the car touching some part
of each other's body, pin her to the hood
and make out like a James Dean movie.
Getting in, she slides across the seat,
straddles your lap and you dry hump
until two half moons form on the icy
windshield and you pry your hand down
the back of her jeans seconds before
she says something about her son, fifteen
minutes, and picking him up from school.

Yes, you are in love, happier than you deserve.
You'll never have to talk to that woman,
or anybody else on the damn train, and learn
that her head's bobbing to the numbing bass
of some electronic dance track crap,
that her dog eared book is a signed copy
of Oprah's biography. No, you can consider
giving up a rent controlled apartment,
moving to Brooklyn. You can worry
about finding less and less time to write,
start to miss your closet full of porn
and wonder how difficult it will be to live
with a seven year old, autistic boy
and that Linda Blair Exorcist sound
he makes whenever he gets upset.
You can remember the last time
you lived with someone, the way
you quickly tired of each other,
how the times between making love
stretched longer and wider until
you rarely touched, the way it still
hurt when she left and how for years
you believed you'd never get over it.

As you step out of the subway,
the light stings your eyes. Buds
are beginning to dot the ends
of branches and girls are wearing
barely any clothing. You walk
the few blocks to work humming
a new Brian Wilson song, remember

how much you loved summer
as a kid. When you cross the street
a car screeches to a stop.
The driver beats on his horn,
leans his head out, starts yelling
in a language you are fortunate
not to understand. You imagine
telling him you're in love,
that you can't help yourself.
You're sorry, but you don't know
what you're doing. He nods, as if
he knows too well what that means,
then drives away. But not before
bestowing on you the blessings
of a God millions believe in.

OPEN HOUSE

It's June and Jaime Luis
is selling Puerto Rican flags
from the trunk of his Bonneville.
Men old enough to be his grandfather
sit in a sliver of shade playing
dominoes. He reaches into
the cooler, digs to the bottom.
Four white girls with no make-up,
no asses, rise out of the subway,
shade their eyes and search
for street signs. The one in the lead
glances at a scrap of paper
in her fist. Jaime Luis
doesn't need to read her lips.

820 Nevins Street, between Warren
and Wyckoff: His cousin's house
until the landlord tripled the rent
last December. They're standing
on the corner, his corner, not sure
which way to go, wondering
if he speaks English, if anyone
remembers their high school
Spanish. He doesn't know
when the rice and beans restaurant
his aunt half owns will turn
into a sushi bar, the Bodega
down the block will become
a Pâtisserie with fresh cut
flowers, tiny sidewalk tables.

But he knows all about August,
its unraveling string of dripping
eighty degree nights, the power
blinking off and on, the next cop
shooting the next unarmed nigga,
and he sees those girls standing
behind their curtains at night,
scurrying to and from the subway
like fucking cockroaches. He steps
toward the women, removes his hat.
"Por favor?" They look at each other,
the ground, before one of them
picks up the smallest flag
and hands him a ten. Without
waiting for change, they walk
away in the wrong direction.

ANTHONY

You know something bad
is about to happen
when you're sitting
in a nearly empty theater
watching a film critics
gave raves, a film you think
is insipid, self-indulgent
and could only be saved
if the utterly beautiful
co-stars quickly stripped
to make mad lesbian love
when this fat Asian guy
squeezes across the row
and sits next to you.

He's breathing fast
and you can smell
spearmint on his breath.
When the screen goes
light gray, you watch
his slick-with-sweat-
slab-of-arm creep over
the arm rest and you grab
your backpack in one
graceless motion, bolt
down the aisle, out
the glass doors.

And all damn day
something's following you,
hovering around your head
like a gnat in tall grass,

94

like the time you didn't
pick up the phone
in the middle of the night
and you let your mom talk
to your machine, go on
and on about your brother
arrested for driving drunk
again. She kept saying
your name, Anthony,
stressing every letter.
Not Antnee. Not Ant.
Yeah, A N T H O N Y
skittering across the floors
in the dark, bouncing off
the bare walls, telling you
to get up and meet her
at the Queens courthouse,
Anthony, in ninety minutes.
Please, Anthony.

You turned over, tried
to fall back to sleep
and for too many days
after, you were sure
everyone was looking
at you, seeing clean
through you. Even
your mother knew
what you did
and didn't do
when you called
two days later,

told her you just
got back from visiting
your girl in Vermont
and asked how did it go,
how's John doing?
And she said who knows,
then got real quiet.
Both of you, not saying
a word, wondering
if she loved you,
still loved you enough
not to call you a liar.

THE WAY A WORLD CAN CHANGE

Start with a letter from a woman
who disappeared, broke
your heart eight years ago.
Her life's a stolen car,
an escape from a cult,
a sperm bank son, six
years old, autistic.
She's not sure why
she's writing. Don't laugh
it says, she's moving
to Vermont, trying to find
herself and she remembers
the time spent with you
as happy, stable.

Read it again. Write back,
edit it like a new poem.
You're working the same
job, there are still no
pictures on your walls,
your first full length collection
will be published in January.
You like the name Joshua, ask
if he has her clear blue eyes.
Hope that when she finds herself
it will be the woman you loved.
Write. Call. Anytime.

Answer the phone. It's her,
Hilary. Talk until Joshua
screams too loud and wrestles

the phone from her hands.
Fly Jet Blue. Kiss
in the garage like kids
at recess. Eat at a diner.
Hold hands, touch knees
under the table. Make love,
fuck on her futon until
it's time to pick up Joshua
from school. Try not
to feel so warm, so lucky.

Eleven months later, Brooklyn.
Hilary, Joshua, you, living
in an apartment you can barely
afford. He's sick, she's left
for her new job and you're half
asleep. The phone rings.
Hilary's crying. She says
to turn the TV on. You watch
the buildings burn and fall,
wish you could hold her
as you feel Joshua's head
for fever. She'll be home
soon as she can. Be careful.
She loves you. Quietly
lie down next to Joshua.

Two nights later, go outside.
The sidewalks are empty,
hushed. Something is still
burning. You hold Hilary's

hand, watch Joshua graze
his fingers against fences.
Flags drape every third
porch. A cat rattles
a trash can, a dog growls
and your neck tenses
with each sound. You pull
Hilary closer. Joshua darts
into Ocean Parkway. A car
swerves, skids to a stop.
The driver drops his head
to the steering wheel,
covers it with his arms,
relieved. She crouches,
cries into his shoulder.
You sit on the curb,
hug your knees.
End here, please.

GETTING AWAY

The kids bicker in the back seat.
They're sick of each other,
these weekends in the Berkshires.
They want to stay home, play
with their friends. Maybe
next week I lie. My wife
sits in the death seat, rolls
down her window, smokes
her cigarette and wonders
if I will ever fix the damn
air conditioner. Construction
narrows the highway to two
slow lanes. The radio
spits the six o'clock news
through static. Sweat slides
down my spine. I grip the stick
in a fist, punch the car closer
to the toll booth, drop quarters
in the basket, and the gate

Lifts. We hit open road. Wind
whips my hair, the DJ spins
"Rosalita." I sing every word:
1979, Erica, her gypsy dresses,
the silver crucifix hanging between
her freckled breasts. The song
ends. I look at my watch, picture
myself unpacking bags, putting
Kate and Jesse to bed. By ten,
I should be sitting on the porch,
my wife's head nesting in my lap
trying to remember the names of stars.

Later, she'll drape her faded jeans
over Grandma Melton's rocking
chair, lie back in bed and shut
her eyes the first time I enter her.
She'll wrap her legs around my back,
move to meet me, and I'll think
only of her until I fall asleep.

WHEN MY WIFE ASKS ME FOR A DIVORCE MY UNCLE JIMMY TAKES ME FOR A WALK AND TALKS ABOUT THE GOOD OLD DAYS

Come on, he says, it's not far.
We can walk to my old school.
If the gate's locked, we'll climb
the fence. Easy. Put your foot
here. Now there. That's it. Up
and over. Lunch time, this yard
was filled with hundreds of kids
skipping rope and flipping baseball
cards, nuns fingering strings
of black beads, pacing like prison
guards. I played punch ball.
The first fifth grader in history
to hit the ball on the roof.

When the bell rang,
we lined up in size place,
entered the building two by two.
No talking. We sat in alphabetical
order, seven rows of ten seats,
our hands folded, reciting
catechism. God made me.
God made me to know, love
and serve him. Talking?
Five whacks of the strap
across your hands. Bathroom?
You kidding? Hold it in.

After school, stickball. Fresh
chalked boxes on brick walls,
scoreboards drawn that looked
like arrows on the ground.

We'd print our names, fill in
all nine innings. Everyone
could tell who won, who lost
until rain came, washed it away.

Dinner, six o'clock sharp.
Fathers made livings
with their hands or backs
while mothers stayed home
to cook and clean and yell
and tell our fathers everything
so they could hit and punish us.
Good men drank weekends
only. Good women never
complained. Daughters married
before they turned twenty,
nine and a half months before
their first child, please Jesus
let it be a boy, was born.
Good sons stayed out of jail,
sometimes finished high school.
Husbands and wives stay
together. In life and in death.
St. Peter meets us at the gate,
points to heaven or hell.
No explanations. No begging.

So, I told your Aunt Mary, no,
I don't understand. You're not
happy and you want to spend
some time apart? You want

to take the kids to your mother's
for a few weeks? I says I'm sorry,
but you and the kids ain't going
nowhere. Now, let's go home.

EASTER 2002

It's Easter morning and I'm up early
folding the mattress back into
the couch. My wife is asleep
behind our closed bedroom door.
My step son is sliding the first
of today's maybe two hundred videos
into the machine's slot. Even though
no one in this apartment has any reason
to believe in Jesus, last night
we pretended everything was good.
Joshua wasn't autistic and Hilary
wasn't falling out of love with me.
We sat at the kitchen table, dipped
hard boiled eggs into plastic cups
filled with colored water. Joshua
crouched, his eyes level with the edge
of the table and he jumped in delight
every time we dunked an egg
beneath the surface. Hilary
caught my eye a few times
and neither one of us could keep
from smiling. When Joshua lost
interest, walked back to his room,
we finished the dozen, hardly
talking. She then said goodnight,
took a book to bed while I played
the radio softly, thought about
the way everything fell apart
so quickly and how helpless
I felt as I bent down, hid
a purple egg under the bed,
leaned over to kiss Joshua
while he slept so perfectly.

ONE YEAR LATER

My brother was on his way
to a dental appointment
when the second plane hit
four stories below the office
where he worked. He's never
said anything about the guy
who took football bets, how
he liked to watch his secretary
walk, the friends he ate lunch with,
all the funerals. Maybe, shamed
by his luck, he keeps quiet,
afraid someone might guess
how good he feels, breathing.

VISITS

Days like this I wish
I was six years old
and autistic, like Joshua,
the way he opens the door
and grabs my hand,
leads me to his room
on my weekly visits.
His mother sits in
the kitchen, her arms
crossed loosely against
her chest, thinking
I guess. He stands on
this special, worn out circle
of rug, says, "One, two, three.
Up, Tony" and I lift him,
throw him high as I can.
He lands on the bed
laughing, and I pounce
on top of him, lie there
until he wraps his arms
around my neck and I ask,
no beg, for just one squeeze,
and he pulls me tighter,
hugs me for less than
an instant. We do this
over and over, both of us
running out of breath, seven,
ten minutes, until he says,
"See you later," walks me
down the hall to the room
where I used to sleep.

If I paid the Spanish lady
with the tiny barking dog
who lives down the hall
to come by once or twice
a week, showed her how
to pick Joshua up, throw
him on the bed exactly
the way I do, I'm not sure
he could tell the difference.
And if I was Joshua
I wouldn't love Hilary
so desperately. Anyone
could take her place:
The tall, pretty teacher
who lives in Jersey, loves
Lucinda Williams, poetry,
Southside Johnny, driving
fast and dancing slow.
The thirty-three year old
with her dark eyes and sexy
mouth, the Thurman Munson
baseball card taped
to her bedroom mirror.
The woman sitting across
the table at my best friend's
wedding. Last weekend,
alone in Baltimore. Someone
said her name was Jackie.
She had this little girl
voice and kept leaning
over as she bit
into soft shell crabs.

GOODBYE

Today, I picked Joshua up
from music group. He said
my name soon as I stepped
through the door, tried to run
to me. The therapist stood
in his way, forced him to stay
until he made eye contact,
said goodbye to her assistant,
the other kids. She slowly
walked him over to me,
assured me how much better
he was doing while he tugged
on my arm repeating 'home'
louder and louder. I thanked her
while we headed out the door,
tried to keep him from jumping
into every puddle, steer him
from bumping into people
as we turned down subway stairs.

Joshua took a window seat,
got on his knees and traced
the outline of his face as we rode.
I finger counted the six stops
to Hamilton Parkway, promised
that his mom would be waiting
for him. When the train rose
out of the ground, climbed up
into the cloudless sky, he ran
to the front door. I stood behind
him, played with his hair as all
of Red Hook spread beneath us.

I glanced at the other riders,
curious whether they could tell
something was wrong with Joshua
then wondered what he was thinking,
if his brain could hold anything
other than shapes and colors
flying past, the feel of glass
against his fingertips, the thought
that his mommy would be waiting
three, now two, stations away.
I imagined what he would do
if we stayed on longer, rode out
to Coney Island. Would he stop
crying and fighting long enough
to see or hear, smell, the ocean?
Would he run across the sand
like the summer before, strip
down to his shorts? Jump
and play in the waves until
the last light left the sky?

The closets are empty
and piles of packed boxes
line the walls of his house,
but I'm not sure Joshua knows
that this means he's moving
back to Vermont in the morning.
I don't know if he can grasp
the concept of missing someone
or understand how hard
it is for me to keep from crying.

He has no idea that I met him
three years ago. I went
with Hilary to pick him up
from school one afternoon.
The Sunday after, finished
with my bowl of oatmeal,
I was watching her lift
her teacup to her lips
when I realized I wanted
to spend my life with her
and it scared me to death.

I don't know what Joshua
remembers about Vermont,
about moving to Brooklyn;
if he knows when things started
to fall apart or why me and his mom
couldn't find a way to stay together;
if he remembers that I moved
down the block, kept visiting him
while everyone I know told me
to let go and move on,
that I didn't owe him a thing,
and no one seemed to accept
or understand I love Joshua,
that the way he will never fit
in the world reminds me of me
and I wish he was my son,
my eight year old boy.
My, my, mine.

FAITH

You find it hard to believe
in any kind of God: Priests,
little boys, countless kept secrets;
Israelis, Palestinians, that dirty war
over somebody's idea of holy land;

Your girlfriend's autistic son,
and how she stopped loving you
suddenly; the sharp, numbing
loneliness. Yet, every morning

You reach across the mattress
quiet that bleating alarm,
sit up, still half asleep,
ready to do whatever
the hell it is you now do.

THE LAST LIE

Now those memories come back to haunt me
They haunt me like a curse
Is a dream a lie if it don't come true
Or is it something worse
Bruce Springsteen, "The River"

I know I've lied before,
tiny white ones, every day
exaggerations and self deprecations
to make me seem deeper and tougher,
simpler and weirder, more self
contained, less ordinary, less like you.
I started young, signed an application,
swore I was nine instead of eight
to play sandlot baseball before
my time. Now, I'll keep quiet
when people think I'm only forty;
but lines are forming beneath
my eyes and my last girlfriend
married a guy half my age.

Once, I lied in a poem,
changed the name of a girl
so no one knew I was the last,
the oldest, guy on my block
to finally get laid. No, I never
got past Julia Jordan's breasts,
not my cock, tongue or finger
even though she was beautiful
in the soft sweet way I always
dreamt about: deep blue
ocean eyes, summer freckles, silky
hair hanging down and brushing
her great ass. Yeah, I loved her
and I knew she wanted to do it

in my parents' basement, the back
of her father's station wagon,
in an Allentown barn, visiting
her space cadet, Jesus freak sister.
But I was as slow and awkward
as a retard, worried and scared
I wouldn't know what to do
and we never could find words
to say anything about any of it.

No, I lied a few years ago
for real. It mattered, broke
somebody's heart and should
never be forgiven. I lied
to the girl I first made love to,
the woman I've loved longest,
the woman who talked
about breaking up her family
because we both believed
we belonged together. Finally.
We were walking down Houston
to see some movie and I said no
I wasn't seeing anyone else.
I looked in her eyes, paid
for two tickets and sat
in the movie dark, slid
my hand under her skirt,
made sure she was wet.

And yeah, I kept lying
after I told her the truth

a day later as she screamed
and cried and cursed me
all the way from Virginia.
I apologized, tried to explain
she was still married, it could
take maybe years before
she could move to New York,
that Suzanne was just someone
to fuck in the meantime. I never
said I didn't want to wait
around for her, that I didn't
believe she would ever leave
her husband or I was already
too much in love with Suzanne.
But she knew and kept away.

We are back in touch now.
She'll sneak off in her car,
use a phone card and call me
on birthdays and her voice
will linger for hours. We'll meet
for dinner when she visits
her parents in Queens, hold
hands, talk about everything.
She tried not to look too happy
when I told her Suzanne married
her old boyfriend in September.
I nod my head when she says
she's so wrapped up in her son
and the every day of life
that she forgets everything

she's missing and I promise
myself I won't lie anymore.
Not about something
like that. Not to her.

TRADING PLACES OR OUT AMONG THE MISSING AND LOST

Maybe I was on the D Train
methodically making my way
to a Yankee Stadium day game
when some legless beggar rolled
slowly through the car holding
a paper cup in his clenched teeth.
While I wondered if he was faking
like Eddie Murphy in Trading Places
or if his legs were really blown to bits
outside a Viet Nam village in 1968,
my friend Dave leaned over, took
a handful of change from his pocket.

I think I thought about India, how
I once heard or read that fathers
would mangle, cut off a limb or two
for added sympathy when their children
were old enough to hit the streets, beg
Americans for money. I couldn't help
but remember when I was five years old,
a cripple with a heavy iron brace strapped
down my left leg, a Frankenstein boot
on my other foot and everybody stared
at poor poor pitiful embarrassed me
as I shut my eyes, tried to disappear
to a place where no one could find me
and taught myself never to ask
for anything from anyone as that guy
raised his eyes, nodded thanks.

I was hoping Pettitte was pitching
as Dave started talking body parts,

which one he'd least like to lose
in a sudden drunk driving accident
or to some unnamed mysterious disease.
When he swore he'd rather die than lose
his cock, we both laughed as the train
chugged toward the Bronx. I don't know
if he was afraid of the pain, worried
about the humiliation of pissing through
a thin tube or whether he was already
missing all the women he imagined
one day fucking, carefully calculating
degrees and fractions of how much
less of a man it would make him feel.
I doubt if he was imagining his wife,
pregnant with hopefully his second son
and all the times lying next to her
wishing he could masturbate in peace.

I'd already realized I'd never get to use
my cock as often as I daydreamed
and I was tired of being worn down
by expectations and unfulfilled promise,
even a few fantasies had come true
and still didn't turn out nearly as good
as I imagined. Besides, I was always
afraid of losing my eyes, my sight
since I stood in the back of first grade
unable to read the eye chart. No,
I couldn't make out that big black E
no matter how hard or often Sister Carolina
hit it with her pointer as the kids

all laughed louder and later made fun
of my thick framed glasses. Even now
when I sleep, I keep a hallway light on,
worried about crazy nightmares, chased
by slow motion zombies and falling
helplessly into the gaping black holes
of where their eye balls should be.

Whenever I see a blind person walking
the streets of NYC with their gentle dog
or tapping and sweeping their cane
as they slowly make their way down
subway steps, I want to follow them
everywhere they go, introduce myself
and ask them question after question
in a too loud, silly sing song tone
about fearlessness and darkness,
what kind of music they like, if
they've lost or found God, how
trapped or angry, crazy and lonely
they feel, if they'd like to hang out,
go for a cup of coffee or tea, find
a bar and drink until we sing karaoke,
get into a brawl, puke and pass out.

Me, I'd probably stay in bed, pray
it wasn't too late to become
an old black Mississippi blues man,
wait for my friends and family
to drop off food and shopping bags
filled with bootleg CDs, listen

to baseball on a tiny transistor radio,
perfect helplessness, wither deeper
into myself and my limited imagination,
miss the things I did, didn't, and will
never get to do, everything I never
watch carefully enough, the ugliness,
the beauty, I turn too quickly away from.
I'd miss everything new and exciting
I somehow might someday stumble upon.

NIECE

Last week, while I was in Vermont visiting
my ex-girlfriend and her twelve year old,
Joshua, my baby brother's wife gave birth
to their first child, a girl, Saturday night.

Today, I'm standing on their Long Island steps
waiting for someone to come to the door.
My brother grabs my jacket, leads me
down the hall with this dazed half smile.

No one in my family knows how to talk
about anything that matters, but our eyes collide
and I want to believe we both recognize
how warm and charged this piece of quiet feels.

His wife walks across the living room carrying
a too pink bundle, humming almost imperceptibly.
She's wearing gray sweats and looks tousled,
softer, more beautiful than I thought possible.

I can't tell if the baby is as pretty as my mother—
delighted to be a grandmother for the third time—
insisted over and over during our long distance call
or if she looks like anyone in anybody's family.

I nod and my brother's wife leans closer, places
the baby in my arms and I can't believe how tiny
this little girl is, how every single finger is a bigger
miracle than anything I've seen in too many years.

Later, while riding the railroad home, I'll count
all the stalled construction projects we glide by,
wonder why I never wanted anything this wonderful
to happen to me, if I'll miss it more the older I get.

I'll think about what Joshua means to me, how easy
it is to be generous, to simply love him unconditionally
from far away and whether I'd turn into myself
become a selfish, impatient, too strict father up close.

But right now, Alexis Leigh is resting in my lap
occasionally yawning and stretching, letting
the pacifier slip out of her mouth and I'm rocking
gently doing all I can to keep her happy.

LEFT BEHIND

These mornings, you're not sure
what will wake you first:
the smell of cigarette smoke
sifting through a window screen,
the hushed voices of men
in hard hats sipping coffee
or the high pitched beep beep
of trucks backing down streets.
You roll out of bed, click off
the alarm a half hour before
it rings. By the time you start
to brush your teeth, jack
hammers are digging deeper
to build higher and keep pace
with rising rents, the changing
neighborhood. It's easy to think
of the late 70's and your grandfather,
the last white man left standing
in Bed Stuy, sitting at the head
of the table with his hands clasped
as if in prayer talking about
his long gone days, complaining
about the coloreds taking over
and your god damn long hair.

You recognize fewer and fewer
people as you walk the ten blocks
to the subway. No need to nod
hello, stop and talk with anyone.
Almost overnight, everyone's grown
younger, thinner, richer, whiter
and they all own dogs or nannies

who commandeer strollers like tanks.
You miss the corner candy store,
the Deli next door and its thick
Italian heroes. The newsstand
still guards the subway entrance.
You went to school with the owner
and you're both scarred by the names
of nuns and Franciscan Brothers
who tried and failed to beat
any sense into you. Head down,
Tom's changing a creased twenty
licking his ink stained fingers.
You're staring at beautiful women
as they buy bottled water, check
cell phones and text messages
to men and boys nothing like you.

Was it the day before yesterday
or as far back as thirty years ago
that you could slam that window
shut and return to bed, lie with Erica,
Suzanne or Hilary and the only things
that entered your mind were breakfast,
whether the local theater was showing
the movie you were dying to see
or maybe you would quietly get up,
step across the room and put on
some sweet soulful morning music
and do it all blessed day long?
She'd rest her head against your
chest, play with your softening cock

and you'd talk about schoolyard days,
books, songs, hitchhiking cross country,
the first time you almost had sex
and how you could stay here forever.
You'd laugh, whisper and sometimes
talk out loud about building your own
world, how everything would fall
into place gracefully, never thinking
about your grandfather easing closer
to death, afraid of feeling left behind.

THIRTEEN

Three states away, Joshua's
celebrating a birthday. All
last week he read social stories
trying to learn what cake, lit
candles, pizza party hats and gifts
are supposed to mean to him.
I play the jumpy email video,
watch as he slides into a booth,
shakes salt into his palm, tilts
his head sideways and like always
his eyes light up as crystals pour
from his fingers like fairy dust.
He makes his infamous shrieking
sound when the teacher hands
him a hat and he doesn't stop
screaming or pounding the table
until she stuffs it in the trash.

A few kids slide in
next to him, across from him
and take turns slapping,
grabbing his hand in different
secret ways and Joshua doesn't
start howling, doesn't try
to hide under the table or yell
for his mom's blue van.
He just covers his mouth
with his hand as he laughs
so hard that goose bumps
start to crawl down my arm.
Patiently he waits for the pizza,

blows the candles out, takes
a slice, nibbles counter clockwise
around its steaming edges,
drinks half a Snapple
and then rips his gifts open.

When I visited last winter,
he spent nearly four hours
repeating "Tony airport bye"
and I wasn't sure he knew me
until the next morning when
he placed his face close to mine.
He put his finger in his mouth,
tried to make the popping sound
I showed him the first time
we met. I remembered
how he'd jump with joy,
crumble into a soft, giggling,
rolling-across-the-floor-ball
every time I did it. He'd grab
my finger, lift it to my lips
and say "Again Tony again."
Later, he sprawled across
my lap, let me rub his feet
as he turned pages of shiny
alphabet books, slid his fingers
over the illustrations like
he was speed reading Braille.

At thirteen, he's bigger, stronger.
He throws clothes, magazines

across his bed, desk and floor
like any teenager and he plays
his MP3 endlessly. Still
he listens to the same six
Sesame Street jingles over
and over. Recently he's pulled
hair, torn shirts, bit teachers
and attacked Hilary in the middle
of the night once. She never
told me how badly he hurt her,
but she's having trouble sleeping
and feels more overwhelmed
than usual. He's started
on a low dose of medication,
but she can't tell how much
it's helping and no one knows
about long term side effects.

I want to book an early
morning flight, drive over
the hills, ride to the rescue
like John Wayne's cavalry.
I want to remember how
much I miss and love both
of them, forget the part
of me that's relieved
I no longer feel guilty
for not spending every hour
of every day trying to cure
his autism, that even if me
and his mom still loved

each other the way we swore
we would, hunkered down
close and deep in our bunkers,
there may never be a way
to make a place in this world
for Joshua or either one of us.

TWENTY-EIGHT

This woman who told me
I was too old for her
said she sometimes wonders
what I was like at 28. Sure,
I was 10-20 pounds thinner
with darker, longer hair
hanging down my back.
But already, I had started
working with retarded
and autistic kids, sending
my poems out, trying to learn
if they had anything to say
to anyone other than me.

I was always quiet, shy
and I probably think
too much, never learned
how to let go and have fun.
I can be self absorbed,
thoughtless, too often sarcastic,
irreverent and hard headed.
And no I never liked parties
or politics or money and most
people. I didn't play guitar,
drive a fast car, never dreamt
of spending a year in Turkey,
Timbuktu, Portugal, a weekend
in the Hamptons or building
a mansion on a hill, filling it
with kids and lovable pets.

Even then, I knew that listening
to 2 minutes and 25 seconds
of Brian Wilson or driving down
a late night highway shouting
along to "Thunder Road" was as good
as I could feel, that the rhythm
of a basketball bouncing past
my Sunday morning window
or a backyard 6 year old
whacking a wiffle ball
with a plastic bat, sliding
into home plate was as close
to God as I would ever get.

But I was always good
at listening and talking
and touching, and when
I was 28, I was in love,
mad-crazy-deep-silly, radio
song, it takes two, you
and me against the world
kind of love and anytime
we sat at a table and broke
bread, spent a rainy weekend
tangled up in light blue sheets
or held hands on the crowded
Monday morning F train
stuck once again in the tunnel
between Queens and Manhattan
I was sure we'd last forever.

At 28, this girl was so in love
with me that her amazing
green-brown eyes would get
all lit up whenever she looked
at me. At 28, I had everything
in the world I ever needed.
At 28, I was just about
as dumb as I am now.

About the Author

Tony Gloeggler was born in Brooklyn, lives in Queens and hopes to die somewhere nearby and somewhat conveniently. He's managed a group home for developmentally disabled men in Boerum Hill for nearly 30 years. His poems have appeared in numerous journals and anthologies and his work has been nominated for the Pushcart Prize. His chapbook *One on One* received the 1998 Pearl Poetry Prize. Pavement Saw Press published his first full length collection, *One Wish Left*, in 2002 and printed a 2nd edition in 2007. *My Other Life* was published by Jane Street Press in 2004 and *Greatest Hits 1984-2009* was put out by Pudding House Publications in 2009.

About NYQ Books™

NYQ Books™ was established in 2009 as an imprint of The New York Quarterly Foundation, Inc. Its mission is to augment the *New York Quarterly* poetry magazine by providing an additional venue for poets already published in the magazine. A lifelong dream of NYQ's founding editor, William Packard, NYQ Books™ has been made possible by both growing foundation support and new technology that was not available during William Packard's lifetime. We are proud to present these books to you and hope that you will continue to support The New York Quarterly Foundation, Inc. and our poets and that you will enjoy these other titles from NYQ Books™:

Joanna Crispi	*Soldier in the Grass*
Ira Joe Fisher	*Songs from an Earlier Century*
Ted Jonathan	*Bones and Jokes*
Fred Yannantuono	*A Boilermaker for the Lady*
Sanford Fraser	*Tourist*
Grace Zabriskie	*Poems*

Please visit our website for these and other titles:

www.nyqbooks.org

Breinigsville, PA USA
20 June 2010
240251BV00001B/93/P